THIS GRATITUDE JOURNAL

JOURNAL

Belongs To:

_____

Practice An
ATTITUDE
of Gratitude

I'm GRATEFUL Every Day

"Gratitude is the fairest blossom which springs from the soul." – Henry Ward Beecher

I'M GRATEFUL FOR: **DATE:**

1. _____
2. _____
3. _____

I'M GRATEFUL FOR: **DATE:**

1. _____
2. _____
3. _____

I'M GRATEFUL FOR: **DATE:**

1. _____
2. _____
3. _____

I'M GRATEFUL FOR: **DATE:**

1. _____

2. _____

3. _____

I'M GRATEFUL FOR: **DATE:**

1. _____

2. _____

3. _____

I'M GRATEFUL FOR: **DATE:**

1. _____

2. _____

3. _____

I'M GRATEFUL FOR: **DATE:**

1. _____

2. _____

3. _____

I'm GRATEFUL Every Day

> *"The sweetest of all sounds is praise."*
> – Xenophon

I'M GRATEFUL FOR:　　　　　　　　　　**DATE:**

1. _____

2. _____

3. _____

I'M GRATEFUL FOR:　　　　　　　　　　**DATE:**

1. _____

2. _____

3. _____

I'M GRATEFUL FOR:　　　　　　　　　　**DATE:**

1. _____

2. _____

3. _____

I'M GRATEFUL FOR: **DATE:**

1. ....

2. ....

3. ....

I'M GRATEFUL FOR: **DATE:**

1. ....

2. ....

3. ....

I'M GRATEFUL FOR: **DATE:**

1. ....

2. ....

3. ....

I'M GRATEFUL FOR: **DATE:**

1. ....

2. ....

3. ....

I'm GRATEFUL Every Day

> *"To be content with what we possess is the greatest and most secure of riches."* – Cicero

---

I'M GRATEFUL FOR: **DATE:**

1. _____
2. _____
3. _____

I'M GRATEFUL FOR: **DATE:**

1. _____
2. _____
3. _____

I'M GRATEFUL FOR: **DATE:**

1. _____
2. _____
3. _____

I'M GRATEFUL FOR: DATE:

1. _____

2. _____

3. _____

I'M GRATEFUL FOR: DATE:

1. _____

2. _____

3. _____

I'M GRATEFUL FOR: DATE:

1. _____

2. _____

3. _____

I'M GRATEFUL FOR: DATE:

1. _____

2. _____

3. _____

I'm GRATEFUL Every Day

> *"I awoke this morning with devout thanksgiving for my friends, the old and new."*
> – Ralph Waldo Emerson

I'M GRATEFUL FOR: **DATE:**

1. _____
2. _____
3. _____

I'M GRATEFUL FOR: **DATE:**

1. _____
2. _____
3. _____

I'M GRATEFUL FOR: **DATE:**

1. _____
2. _____
3. _____

I'M GRATEFUL FOR: **DATE:**

1. _____

2. _____

3. _____

I'M GRATEFUL FOR: **DATE:**

1. _____

2. _____

3. _____

I'M GRATEFUL FOR: **DATE:**

1. _____

2. _____

3. _____

I'M GRATEFUL FOR: **DATE:**

1. _____

2. _____

3. _____

I'm GRATEFUL Every Day

> *"Gratitude turns what we have into enough."*
> – Anonymous

I'M GRATEFUL FOR: **DATE:**

1. _____

2. _____

3. _____

I'M GRATEFUL FOR: **DATE:**

1. _____

2. _____

3. _____

I'M GRATEFUL FOR: **DATE:**

1. _____

2. _____

3. _____

I'M GRATEFUL FOR: **DATE:**

1. _____

2. _____

3. _____

I'M GRATEFUL FOR: **DATE:**

1. _____

2. _____

3. _____

I'M GRATEFUL FOR: **DATE:**

1. _____

2. _____

3. _____

I'M GRATEFUL FOR: **DATE:**

1. _____

2. _____

3. _____

I'm GRATEFUL Every Day

"Gratitude is not only the greatest of virtues but the parent of all others." – Cicero

I'M GRATEFUL FOR: **DATE:**

1. ....
2. ....
3. ....

I'M GRATEFUL FOR: **DATE:**

1. ....
2. ....
3. ....

I'M GRATEFUL FOR: **DATE:**

1. ....
2. ....
3. ....

I'M GRATEFUL FOR: **DATE:**

1. _____

2. _____

3. _____

I'M GRATEFUL FOR: **DATE:**

1. _____

2. _____

3. _____

I'M GRATEFUL FOR: **DATE:**

1. _____

2. _____

3. _____

I'M GRATEFUL FOR: **DATE:**

1. _____

2. _____

3. _____

I'm GRATEFUL Every Day

> *"Thankfulness is the beginning of gratitude.*
> *Gratitude is the completion of thankfulness.*
> *Thankfulness may consist merely of words.*
> *Gratitude is shown in acts."* – Henri Frederic Amiel

I'M GRATEFUL FOR: **DATE:**

1. _____

2. _____

3. _____

I'M GRATEFUL FOR: **DATE:**

1. _____

2. _____

3. _____

I'M GRATEFUL FOR: **DATE:**

1. _____

2. _____

3. _____

I'M GRATEFUL FOR: **DATE:**

1. ....

2. ....

3. ....

I'M GRATEFUL FOR: **DATE:**

1. ....

2. ....

3. ....

I'M GRATEFUL FOR: **DATE:**

1. ....

2. ....

3. ....

I'M GRATEFUL FOR: **DATE:**

1. ....

2. ....

3. ....

I'm GRATEFUL Every Day

> *"In ordinary life, we hardly realize that we receive a great deal more than we give, and that it is only with gratitude that life becomes rich."* – Dietrich Bonhoeffer

I'M GRATEFUL FOR: **DATE:**

1. _____

2. _____

3. _____

I'M GRATEFUL FOR: **DATE:**

1. _____

2. _____

3. _____

I'M GRATEFUL FOR: **DATE:**

1. _____

2. _____

3. _____

I'M GRATEFUL FOR: DATE:

1.

2.

3.

I'M GRATEFUL FOR: DATE:

1.

2.

3.

I'M GRATEFUL FOR: DATE:

1.

2.

3.

I'M GRATEFUL FOR: DATE:

1.

2.

3.

I'm GRATEFUL Every Day

"No one who achieves success does so without the help of others. The wise and confident acknowledge this help with gratitude." – Alfred North Whitehead

I'M GRATEFUL FOR: **DATE:**

1. ....

2. ....

3. ....

I'M GRATEFUL FOR: **DATE:**

1. ....

2. ....

3. ....

I'M GRATEFUL FOR: **DATE:**

1. ....

2. ....

3. ....

I'M GRATEFUL FOR: **DATE:**

1. _____

2. _____

3. _____

I'M GRATEFUL FOR: **DATE:**

1. _____

2. _____

3. _____

I'M GRATEFUL FOR: **DATE:**

1. _____

2. _____

3. _____

I'M GRATEFUL FOR: **DATE:**

1. _____

2. _____

3. _____

I'm GRATEFUL Every Day

"I would maintain that thanks are the highest form of thought, and that gratitude is happiness doubled by wonder." – Gilbert K. Chesterton

I'M GRATEFUL FOR: **DATE:**

1. _____
2. _____
3. _____

I'M GRATEFUL FOR: **DATE:**

1. _____
2. _____
3. _____

I'M GRATEFUL FOR: **DATE:**

1. _____
2. _____
3. _____

I'M GRATEFUL FOR: **DATE:**

1. _____

2. _____

3. _____

I'M GRATEFUL FOR: **DATE:**

1. _____

2. _____

3. _____

I'M GRATEFUL FOR: **DATE:**

1. _____

2. _____

3. _____

I'M GRATEFUL FOR: **DATE:**

1. _____

2. _____

3. _____

I'm GRATEFUL Every Day

"Two kinds of gratitude: The sudden kind we feel for what we take; the larger kind we feel for what we give." – Edwin Arlington Robinson

I'M GRATEFUL FOR: **DATE:**

1. _____

2. _____

3. _____

I'M GRATEFUL FOR: **DATE:**

1. _____

2. _____

3. _____

I'M GRATEFUL FOR: **DATE:**

1. _____

2. _____

3. _____

I'M GRATEFUL FOR: DATE:

1. _____
2. _____
3. _____

I'M GRATEFUL FOR: DATE:

1. _____
2. _____
3. _____

I'M GRATEFUL FOR: DATE:

1. _____
2. _____
3. _____

I'M GRATEFUL FOR: DATE:

1. _____
2. _____
3. _____

I'm GRATEFUL Every Day

> *"The deepest craving of human nature is the need to be appreciated."* – William James

I'M GRATEFUL FOR: **DATE:**

1. ....

2. ....

3. ....

I'M GRATEFUL FOR: **DATE:**

1. ....

2. ....

3. ....

I'M GRATEFUL FOR: **DATE:**

1. ....

2. ....

3. ....

I'M GRATEFUL FOR: **DATE:**

1. _____

2. _____

3. _____

I'M GRATEFUL FOR: **DATE:**

1. _____

2. _____

3. _____

I'M GRATEFUL FOR: **DATE:**

1. _____

2. _____

3. _____

I'M GRATEFUL FOR: **DATE:**

1. _____

2. _____

3. _____

I'm GRATEFUL Every Day

> *"I've had a remarkable life. I seem to be in such good places at the right time. You know, if you were to ask me to sum my life up in one word, gratitude."* – Dietrich Bonhoeffer

I'M GRATEFUL FOR: **DATE:**

1. _____

2. _____

3. _____

I'M GRATEFUL FOR: **DATE:**

1. _____

2. _____

3. _____

I'M GRATEFUL FOR: **DATE:**

1. _____

2. _____

3. _____

I'M GRATEFUL FOR: **DATE:**

1. ....

2. ....

3. ....

I'M GRATEFUL FOR: **DATE:**

1. ....

2. ....

3. ....

I'M GRATEFUL FOR: **DATE:**

1. ....

2. ....

3. ....

I'M GRATEFUL FOR: **DATE:**

1. ....

2. ....

3. ....

I'm GRATEFUL Every Day

"He is a wise man who does not grieve for the things which he has not, but rejoices for those which he has." – Epictetus

I'M GRATEFUL FOR: **DATE:**

1. _____

2. _____

3. _____

I'M GRATEFUL FOR: **DATE:**

1. _____

2. _____

3. _____

I'M GRATEFUL FOR: **DATE:**

1. _____

2. _____

3. _____

I'M GRATEFUL FOR: DATE:

1. _____

2. _____

3. _____

I'M GRATEFUL FOR: DATE:

1. _____

2. _____

3. _____

I'M GRATEFUL FOR: DATE:

1. _____

2. _____

3. _____

I'M GRATEFUL FOR: DATE:

1. _____

2. _____

3. _____

I'm GRATEFUL Every Day

"Today I choose to live with gratitude for the love that fills my heart, the peace that rests within my spirit, and the voice of hope that says all things are possible." – Anonymous

I'M GRATEFUL FOR: **DATE:**

1. _____

2. _____

3. _____

I'M GRATEFUL FOR: **DATE:**

1. _____

2. _____

3. _____

I'M GRATEFUL FOR: **DATE:**

1. _____

2. _____

3. _____

I'M GRATEFUL FOR: **DATE:**

1. _____
2. _____
3. _____

I'M GRATEFUL FOR: **DATE:**

1. _____
2. _____
3. _____

I'M GRATEFUL FOR: **DATE:**

1. _____
2. _____
3. _____

I'M GRATEFUL FOR: **DATE:**

1. _____
2. _____
3. _____

I'm GRATEFUL Every Day

"Gratitude is the sign of noble souls." – Aesop

I'M GRATEFUL FOR: **DATE:**

1. _____

2. _____

3. _____

I'M GRATEFUL FOR: **DATE:**

1. _____

2. _____

3. _____

I'M GRATEFUL FOR: **DATE:**

1. _____

2. _____

3. _____

I'M GRATEFUL FOR: DATE:

1. _____
2. _____
3. _____

I'M GRATEFUL FOR: DATE:

1. _____
2. _____
3. _____

I'M GRATEFUL FOR: DATE:

1. _____
2. _____
3. _____

I'M GRATEFUL FOR: DATE:

1. _____
2. _____
3. _____

I'm GRATEFUL Every Day

"Nothing is more honorable than a grateful heart." – Seneca the Younger

I'M GRATEFUL FOR: **DATE:**

1. _____

2. _____

3. _____

I'M GRATEFUL FOR: **DATE:**

1. _____

2. _____

3. _____

I'M GRATEFUL FOR: **DATE:**

1. _____

2. _____

3. _____

I'M GRATEFUL FOR: **DATE:**

1.
2.
3.

I'M GRATEFUL FOR: **DATE:**

1.
2.
3.

I'M GRATEFUL FOR: **DATE:**

1.
2.
3.

I'M GRATEFUL FOR: **DATE:**

1.
2.
3.

I'm GRATEFUL Every Day

"If a fellow isn't thankful for what he's got, he isn't likely to be thankful for what he's going to get." – Frank A. Clark

I'M GRATEFUL FOR:	DATE:

1. _____

2. _____

3. _____

I'M GRATEFUL FOR:	DATE:

1. _____

2. _____

3. _____

I'M GRATEFUL FOR:	DATE:

1. _____

2. _____

3. _____

I'M GRATEFUL FOR: DATE:

1. ....

2. ....

3. ....

I'M GRATEFUL FOR: DATE:

1. ....

2. ....

3. ....

I'M GRATEFUL FOR: DATE:

1. ....

2. ....

3. ....

I'M GRATEFUL FOR: DATE:

1. ....

2. ....

3. ....

I'm GRATEFUL Every Day

"When it comes to life the critical thing is whether you take things for granted or take them with gratitude." — G.K. Chesterton

I'M GRATEFUL FOR: **DATE:**

1. _____

2. _____

3. _____

I'M GRATEFUL FOR: **DATE:**

1. _____

2. _____

3. _____

I'M GRATEFUL FOR: **DATE:**

1. _____

2. _____

3. _____

I'M GRATEFUL FOR: **DATE:**

1. _____

2. _____

3. _____

I'M GRATEFUL FOR: **DATE:**

1. _____

2. _____

3. _____

I'M GRATEFUL FOR: **DATE:**

1. _____

2. _____

3. _____

I'M GRATEFUL FOR: **DATE:**

1. _____

2. _____

3. _____

I'm GRATEFUL Every Day

> *"If you want to be on speaking terms with happiness, learn the language of gratitude."*
> – Unknown

I'M GRATEFUL FOR: **DATE:**

1. _____

2. _____

3. _____

I'M GRATEFUL FOR: **DATE:**

1. _____

2. _____

3. _____

I'M GRATEFUL FOR: **DATE:**

1. _____

2. _____

3. _____

I'M GRATEFUL FOR: DATE:

1. ....

2. ....

3. ....

I'M GRATEFUL FOR: DATE:

1. ....

2. ....

3. ....

I'M GRATEFUL FOR: DATE:

1. ....

2. ....

3. ....

I'M GRATEFUL FOR: DATE:

1. ....

2. ....

3. ....

I'm GRATEFUL Every Day

"There is always, always, always something to be thankful for." – Unknown

I'M GRATEFUL FOR: **DATE:**

1. _____
2. _____
3. _____

I'M GRATEFUL FOR: **DATE:**

1. _____
2. _____
3. _____

I'M GRATEFUL FOR: **DATE:**

1. _____
2. _____
3. _____

I'M GRATEFUL FOR: **DATE:**

1.
2.
3.

I'M GRATEFUL FOR: **DATE:**

1.
2.
3.

I'M GRATEFUL FOR: **DATE:**

1.
2.
3.

I'M GRATEFUL FOR: **DATE:**

1.
2.
3.

I'm GRATEFUL Every Day

"Gratitude is a quality similar to electricity: it must be produced and discharged and used up in order to exist at all." – William Faulkner

I'M GRATEFUL FOR: **DATE:**

1. _____
2. _____
3. _____

I'M GRATEFUL FOR: **DATE:**

1. _____
2. _____
3. _____

I'M GRATEFUL FOR: **DATE:**

1. _____
2. _____
3. _____

I'M GRATEFUL FOR: DATE:

1. _____

2. _____

3. _____

I'M GRATEFUL FOR: DATE:

1. _____

2. _____

3. _____

I'M GRATEFUL FOR: DATE:

1. _____

2. _____

3. _____

I'M GRATEFUL FOR: DATE:

1. _____

2. _____

3. _____

I'm GRATEFUL Every Day

"If you haven't all the things you want, be grateful for the things you don't have that you wouldn't want." – Unknown

I'M GRATEFUL FOR: **DATE:**

1. _____
2. _____
3. _____

I'M GRATEFUL FOR: **DATE:**

1. _____
2. _____
3. _____

I'M GRATEFUL FOR: **DATE:**

1. _____
2. _____
3. _____

I'M GRATEFUL FOR: **DATE:**

1. _____

2. _____

3. _____

I'M GRATEFUL FOR: **DATE:**

1. _____

2. _____

3. _____

I'M GRATEFUL FOR: **DATE:**

1. _____

2. _____

3. _____

I'M GRATEFUL FOR: **DATE:**

1. _____

2. _____

3. _____

I'm GRATEFUL Every Day

> *"Swift gratitude is the sweetest."*
> – Greek Proverb

I'M GRATEFUL FOR: **DATE:**

1. _____
2. _____
3. _____

I'M GRATEFUL FOR: **DATE:**

1. _____
2. _____
3. _____

I'M GRATEFUL FOR: **DATE:**

1. _____
2. _____
3. _____

I'M GRATEFUL FOR: **DATE:**

1. _____

2. _____

3. _____

I'M GRATEFUL FOR: **DATE:**

1. _____

2. _____

3. _____

I'M GRATEFUL FOR: **DATE:**

1. _____

2. _____

3. _____

I'M GRATEFUL FOR: **DATE:**

1. _____

2. _____

3. _____

I'm GRATEFUL Every Day

"It's not happiness that brings us gratitude. It's gratitude that brings us happiness."
— Anonymous

I'M GRATEFUL FOR: **DATE:**

1. _____

2. _____

3. _____

I'M GRATEFUL FOR: **DATE:**

1. _____

2. _____

3. _____

I'M GRATEFUL FOR: **DATE:**

1. _____

2. _____

3. _____

I'M GRATEFUL FOR: DATE:

1. _____

2. _____

3. _____

I'M GRATEFUL FOR: DATE:

1. _____

2. _____

3. _____

I'M GRATEFUL FOR: DATE:

1. _____

2. _____

3. _____

I'M GRATEFUL FOR: DATE:

1. _____

2. _____

3. _____

I'm GRATEFUL Every Day

"Appreciation is a wonderful thing: It makes what is excellent in others belong to us as well." — Voltaire

I'M GRATEFUL FOR: **DATE:**

1. _____

2. _____

3. _____

I'M GRATEFUL FOR: **DATE:**

1. _____

2. _____

3. _____

I'M GRATEFUL FOR: **DATE:**

1. _____

2. _____

3. _____

I'M GRATEFUL FOR: DATE:

1. ....

2. ....

3. ....

I'M GRATEFUL FOR: DATE:

1. ....

2. ....

3. ....

I'M GRATEFUL FOR: DATE:

1. ....

2. ....

3. ....

I'M GRATEFUL FOR: DATE:

1. ....

2. ....

3. ....

I'm GRATEFUL Every Day

"Forget injuries, never forget kindnesses."
— Confucius

I'M GRATEFUL FOR: **DATE:**

1. ....

2. ....

3. ....

I'M GRATEFUL FOR: **DATE:**

1. ....

2. ....

3. ....

I'M GRATEFUL FOR: **DATE:**

1. ....

2. ....

3. ....

I'M GRATEFUL FOR: **DATE:**

1. ....

2. ....

3. ....

I'M GRATEFUL FOR: **DATE:**

1. ....

2. ....

3. ....

I'M GRATEFUL FOR: **DATE:**

1. ....

2. ....

3. ....

I'M GRATEFUL FOR: **DATE:**

1. ....

2. ....

3. ....

I'm GRATEFUL Every Day

"The roots of all goodness lie in the soil of appreciation for goodness." — Dalai Lama

I'M GRATEFUL FOR: **DATE:**

1. ....

2. ....

3. ....

I'M GRATEFUL FOR: **DATE:**

1. ....

2. ....

3. ....

I'M GRATEFUL FOR: **DATE:**

1. ....

2. ....

3. ....

I'M GRATEFUL FOR: DATE:

1. _____

2. _____

3. _____

I'M GRATEFUL FOR: DATE:

1. _____

2. _____

3. _____

I'M GRATEFUL FOR: DATE:

1. _____

2. _____

3. _____

I'M GRATEFUL FOR: DATE:

1. _____

2. _____

3. _____

I'm GRATEFUL Every Day

"There are always flowers for those who want to see them." — Henri Matisse

I'M GRATEFUL FOR: **DATE:**

1.
2.
3.

I'M GRATEFUL FOR: **DATE:**

1.
2.
3.

I'M GRATEFUL FOR: **DATE:**

1.
2.
3.

I'M GRATEFUL FOR: DATE:

1. _____
2. _____
3. _____

I'M GRATEFUL FOR: DATE:

1. _____
2. _____
3. _____

I'M GRATEFUL FOR: DATE:

1. _____
2. _____
3. _____

I'M GRATEFUL FOR: DATE:

1. _____
2. _____
3. _____

I'm GRATEFUL Every Day

"We all face difficulties but some of us are grateful that they aren't worse." – Oscar Wilde

I'M GRATEFUL FOR: **DATE:**

1. ....

2. ....

3. ....

I'M GRATEFUL FOR: **DATE:**

1. ....

2. ....

3. ....

I'M GRATEFUL FOR: **DATE:**

1. ....

2. ....

3. ....

I'M GRATEFUL FOR: **DATE:**

1. ....

2. ....

3. ....

I'M GRATEFUL FOR: **DATE:**

1. ....

2. ....

3. ....

I'M GRATEFUL FOR: **DATE:**

1. ....

2. ....

3. ....

I'M GRATEFUL FOR: **DATE:**

1. ....

2. ....

3. ....

I'm GRATEFUL Every Day

"Reflect upon your present blessings of which every man has many - not on your past misfortunes, of which all men have some."
– Charles Dickens

I'M GRATEFUL FOR: **DATE:**

1. _____

2. _____

3. _____

I'M GRATEFUL FOR: **DATE:**

1. _____

2. _____

3. _____

I'M GRATEFUL FOR: **DATE:**

1. _____

2. _____

3. _____

I'M GRATEFUL FOR: **DATE:**

1. _____

2. _____

3. _____

I'M GRATEFUL FOR: **DATE:**

1. _____

2. _____

3. _____

I'M GRATEFUL FOR: **DATE:**

1. _____

2. _____

3. _____

I'M GRATEFUL FOR: **DATE:**

1. _____

2. _____

3. _____

I'm GRATEFUL Every Day

> *"Gratitude is a virtue that has commonly profit annexed to it."* – Epicurus

I'M GRATEFUL FOR: **DATE:**

1. _____

2. _____

3. _____

I'M GRATEFUL FOR: **DATE:**

1. _____

2. _____

3. _____

I'M GRATEFUL FOR: **DATE:**

1. _____

2. _____

3. _____

I'M GRATEFUL FOR: **DATE:**

1. _____

2. _____

3. _____

I'M GRATEFUL FOR: **DATE:**

1. _____

2. _____

3. _____

I'M GRATEFUL FOR: **DATE:**

1. _____

2. _____

3. _____

I'M GRATEFUL FOR: **DATE:**

1. _____

2. _____

3. _____

I'm GRATEFUL Every Day

> *"I can no other answer make, but, thanks, and thanks."* – William Shakespeare

I'M GRATEFUL FOR: **DATE:**

1. _____
2. _____
3. _____

I'M GRATEFUL FOR: **DATE:**

1. _____
2. _____
3. _____

I'M GRATEFUL FOR: **DATE:**

1. _____
2. _____
3. _____

I'M GRATEFUL FOR: **DATE:**

1. ....

2. ....

3. ....

I'M GRATEFUL FOR: **DATE:**

1. ....

2. ....

3. ....

I'M GRATEFUL FOR: **DATE:**

1. ....

2. ....

3. ....

I'M GRATEFUL FOR: **DATE:**

1. ....

2. ....

3. ....

I'm GRATEFUL Every Day

> *"All that we behold is full of blessings."*
> – William Wordsworth

I'M GRATEFUL FOR: **DATE:**

1. _____

2. _____

3. _____

I'M GRATEFUL FOR: **DATE:**

1. _____

2. _____

3. _____

I'M GRATEFUL FOR: **DATE:**

1. _____

2. _____

3. _____

I'M GRATEFUL FOR: **DATE:**

1. _____

2. _____

3. _____

I'M GRATEFUL FOR: **DATE:**

1. _____

2. _____

3. _____

I'M GRATEFUL FOR: **DATE:**

1. _____

2. _____

3. _____

I'M GRATEFUL FOR: **DATE:**

1. _____

2. _____

3. _____

I'm GRATEFUL Every Day

"Be grateful for the moment." – Anonymous

I'M GRATEFUL FOR: **DATE:**

1. _____
2. _____
3. _____

I'M GRATEFUL FOR: **DATE:**

1. _____
2. _____
3. _____

I'M GRATEFUL FOR: **DATE:**

1. _____
2. _____
3. _____

I'M GRATEFUL FOR: **DATE:**

1. _____

2. _____

3. _____

I'M GRATEFUL FOR: **DATE:**

1. _____

2. _____

3. _____

I'M GRATEFUL FOR: **DATE:**

1. _____

2. _____

3. _____

I'M GRATEFUL FOR: **DATE:**

1. _____

2. _____

3. _____

I'm GRATEFUL Every Day

"The greatest blessings of mankind are within us and within our reach. A wise man is content with his lot, whatever it may be, without wishing for what he has not."— Seneca

I'M GRATEFUL FOR: **DATE:**

1. _____

2. _____

3. _____

I'M GRATEFUL FOR: **DATE:**

1. _____

2. _____

3. _____

I'M GRATEFUL FOR: **DATE:**

1. _____

2. _____

3. _____

I'M GRATEFUL FOR: **DATE:**

1. _____

2. _____

3. _____

I'M GRATEFUL FOR: **DATE:**

1. _____

2. _____

3. _____

I'M GRATEFUL FOR: **DATE:**

1. _____

2. _____

3. _____

I'M GRATEFUL FOR: **DATE:**

1. _____

2. _____

3. _____

I'm GRATEFUL Every Day

"No duty is more urgent than that of returning thanks."— James Allen

I'M GRATEFUL FOR: **DATE:**

1. _____

2. _____

3. _____

I'M GRATEFUL FOR: **DATE:**

1. _____

2. _____

3. _____

I'M GRATEFUL FOR: **DATE:**

1. _____

2. _____

3. _____

I'M GRATEFUL FOR: **DATE:**

1. _____
2. _____
3. _____

I'M GRATEFUL FOR: **DATE:**

1. _____
2. _____
3. _____

I'M GRATEFUL FOR: **DATE:**

1. _____
2. _____
3. _____

I'M GRATEFUL FOR: **DATE:**

1. _____
2. _____
3. _____

I'm GRATEFUL Every Day

> *"I would maintain that thanks are the highest form of thought and that gratitude is happiness doubled by wonder."* — Gilbert K. Chesterton

I'M GRATEFUL FOR: **DATE:**

1. _____

2. _____

3. _____

I'M GRATEFUL FOR: **DATE:**

1. _____

2. _____

3. _____

I'M GRATEFUL FOR: **DATE:**

1. _____

2. _____

3. _____

I'M GRATEFUL FOR: **DATE:**

1. ....

2. ....

3. ....

I'M GRATEFUL FOR: **DATE:**

1. ....

2. ....

3. ....

I'M GRATEFUL FOR: **DATE:**

1. ....

2. ....

3. ....

I'M GRATEFUL FOR: **DATE:**

1. ....

2. ....

3. ....

I'm GRATEFUL Every Day

> *"Be grateful for what you have and work hard for what you don't have."*— Anonymous

I'M GRATEFUL FOR:　　　　　　　　　　　　**DATE:**

1. _____

2. _____

3. _____

I'M GRATEFUL FOR:　　　　　　　　　　　　**DATE:**

1. _____

2. _____

3. _____

I'M GRATEFUL FOR:　　　　　　　　　　　　**DATE:**

1. _____

2. _____

3. _____

I'M GRATEFUL FOR: **DATE:**

1. _____

2. _____

3. _____

I'M GRATEFUL FOR: **DATE:**

1. _____

2. _____

3. _____

I'M GRATEFUL FOR: **DATE:**

1. _____

2. _____

3. _____

I'M GRATEFUL FOR: **DATE:**

1. _____

2. _____

3. _____

I'm GRATEFUL Every Day

> *"So much has been given to me; I have no time to ponder over that which has been denied."*
> — Helen Keller

I'M GRATEFUL FOR: **DATE:**

1. _____

2. _____

3. _____

I'M GRATEFUL FOR: **DATE:**

1. _____

2. _____

3. _____

I'M GRATEFUL FOR: **DATE:**

1. _____

2. _____

3. _____

I'M GRATEFUL FOR: **DATE:**

1. _____

2. _____

3. _____

I'M GRATEFUL FOR: **DATE:**

1. _____

2. _____

3. _____

I'M GRATEFUL FOR: **DATE:**

1. _____

2. _____

3. _____

I'M GRATEFUL FOR: **DATE:**

1. _____

2. _____

3. _____

I'm GRATEFUL Every Day

"Let us be grateful to the people who make us happy; they are the charming gardeners who make our souls blossom."— Marcel Proust

I'M GRATEFUL FOR: **DATE:**

1. _____

2. _____

3. _____

I'M GRATEFUL FOR: **DATE:**

1. _____

2. _____

3. _____

I'M GRATEFUL FOR: **DATE:**

1. _____

2. _____

3. _____

I'M GRATEFUL FOR: DATE:

1. ....

2. ....

3. ....

I'M GRATEFUL FOR: DATE:

1. ....

2. ....

3. ....

I'M GRATEFUL FOR: DATE:

1. ....

2. ....

3. ....

I'M GRATEFUL FOR: DATE:

1. ....

2. ....

3. ....

I'm GRATEFUL Every Day

> "The thankful receiver bears a plentiful harvest." – William Blake

I'M GRATEFUL FOR: DATE:

1.
2.
3.

I'M GRATEFUL FOR: DATE:

1.
2.
3.

I'M GRATEFUL FOR: DATE:

1.
2.
3.

I'M GRATEFUL FOR: **DATE:**

1. ....

2. ....

3. ....

I'M GRATEFUL FOR: **DATE:**

1. ....

2. ....

3. ....

I'M GRATEFUL FOR: **DATE:**

1. ....

2. ....

3. ....

I'M GRATEFUL FOR: **DATE:**

1. ....

2. ....

3. ....

I'm GRATEFUL Every Day

> *"Gratitude bestows reverence.....changing forever how we experience life and the world."*
> – John Milton

I'M GRATEFUL FOR: **DATE:**

1. ....

2. ....

3. ....

I'M GRATEFUL FOR: **DATE:**

1. ....

2. ....

3. ....

I'M GRATEFUL FOR: **DATE:**

1. ....

2. ....

3. ....

I'M GRATEFUL FOR: **DATE:**

1. ....

2. ....

3. ....

I'M GRATEFUL FOR: **DATE:**

1. ....

2. ....

3. ....

I'M GRATEFUL FOR: **DATE:**

1. ....

2. ....

3. ....

I'M GRATEFUL FOR: **DATE:**

1. ....

2. ....

3. ....

I'm GRATEFUL Every Day

"Gratitude unlocks the fullness of life."
– Anonymous

I'M GRATEFUL FOR: **DATE:**

1. ....

2. ....

3. ....

I'M GRATEFUL FOR: **DATE:**

1. ....

2. ....

3. ....

I'M GRATEFUL FOR: **DATE:**

1. ....

2. ....

3. ....

I'M GRATEFUL FOR: **DATE:**

1. _____

2. _____

3. _____

I'M GRATEFUL FOR: **DATE:**

1. _____

2. _____

3. _____

I'M GRATEFUL FOR: **DATE:**

1. _____

2. _____

3. _____

I'M GRATEFUL FOR: **DATE:**

1. _____

2. _____

3. _____

I'm GRATEFUL Every Day

> *"Gratitude is the inward feeling of kindness received. Thankfulness is the natural impulse to express that feeling. Thanksgiving is the following of that impulse."* – Henry Van Dyke

I'M GRATEFUL FOR: **DATE:**

1. _____

2. _____

3. _____

I'M GRATEFUL FOR: **DATE:**

1. _____

2. _____

3. _____

I'M GRATEFUL FOR: **DATE:**

1. _____

2. _____

3. _____

I'M GRATEFUL FOR: **DATE:**

1. ....

2. ....

3. ....

I'M GRATEFUL FOR: **DATE:**

1. ....

2. ....

3. ....

I'M GRATEFUL FOR: **DATE:**

1. ....

2. ....

3. ....

I'M GRATEFUL FOR: **DATE:**

1. ....

2. ....

3. ....

I'm GRATEFUL Every Day

> *"If the only prayer you say in your life is "thank you," that would suffice."*
> – Meister Eckhart

I'M GRATEFUL FOR: **DATE:**

1. _____

2. _____

3. _____

I'M GRATEFUL FOR: **DATE:**

1. _____

2. _____

3. _____

I'M GRATEFUL FOR: **DATE:**

1. _____

2. _____

3. _____

I'M GRATEFUL FOR: **DATE:**

1. _____

2. _____

3. _____

I'M GRATEFUL FOR: **DATE:**

1. _____

2. _____

3. _____

I'M GRATEFUL FOR: **DATE:**

1. _____

2. _____

3. _____

I'M GRATEFUL FOR: **DATE:**

1. _____

2. _____

3. _____

I'm GRATEFUL Every Day

> *"A grateful mind is a great mind which eventually attracts to itself great things."* – Plato

I'M GRATEFUL FOR: **DATE:**

1. _____
2. _____
3. _____

I'M GRATEFUL FOR: **DATE:**

1. _____
2. _____
3. _____

I'M GRATEFUL FOR: **DATE:**

1. _____
2. _____
3. _____

I'M GRATEFUL FOR: **DATE:**

1. ....

2. ....

3. ....

I'M GRATEFUL FOR: **DATE:**

1. ....

2. ....

3. ....

I'M GRATEFUL FOR: **DATE:**

1. ....

2. ....

3. ....

I'M GRATEFUL FOR: **DATE:**

1. ....

2. ....

3. ....

I'm GRATEFUL Every Day

"He who receives a good turn should never forget it; he who does one should never remember it." — Proverb

---

I'M GRATEFUL FOR: **DATE:**

1. _____

2. _____

3. _____

I'M GRATEFUL FOR: **DATE:**

1. _____

2. _____

3. _____

I'M GRATEFUL FOR: **DATE:**

1. _____

2. _____

3. _____

I'M GRATEFUL FOR: DATE:

1. _____

2. _____

3. _____

I'M GRATEFUL FOR: DATE:

1. _____

2. _____

3. _____

I'M GRATEFUL FOR: DATE:

1. _____

2. _____

3. _____

I'M GRATEFUL FOR: DATE:

1. _____

2. _____

3. _____

I'm GRATEFUL Every Day

"Persons thankful for little things are certain to be the ones with much to be thankful for."
– Frank Clark

I'M GRATEFUL FOR: **DATE:**

1. ....

2. ....

3. ....

I'M GRATEFUL FOR: **DATE:**

1. ....

2. ....

3. ....

I'M GRATEFUL FOR: **DATE:**

1. ....

2. ....

3. ....

I'M GRATEFUL FOR: DATE:

1. _____

2. _____

3. _____

I'M GRATEFUL FOR: DATE:

1. _____

2. _____

3. _____

I'M GRATEFUL FOR: DATE:

1. _____

2. _____

3. _____

I'M GRATEFUL FOR: DATE:

1. _____

2. _____

3. _____

I'm GRATEFUL Every Day

"Gratitude is the heart's money."
– French Proverb

I'M GRATEFUL FOR: **DATE:**

1. _____

2. _____

3. _____

I'M GRATEFUL FOR: **DATE:**

1. _____

2. _____

3. _____

I'M GRATEFUL FOR: **DATE:**

1. _____

2. _____

3. _____

I'M GRATEFUL FOR: DATE:

1. ....

2. ....

3. ....

I'M GRATEFUL FOR: DATE:

1. ....

2. ....

3. ....

I'M GRATEFUL FOR: DATE:

1. ....

2. ....

3. ....

I'M GRATEFUL FOR: DATE:

1. ....

2. ....

3. ....

I'm GRATEFUL Every Day

> *"As we express our gratitude, we must never forget that the highest appreciation is not to utter words, but to live by them."*
> – John F. Kennedy

I'M GRATEFUL FOR: **DATE:**

1. ....

2. ....

3. ....

I'M GRATEFUL FOR: **DATE:**

1. ....

2. ....

3. ....

I'M GRATEFUL FOR: **DATE:**

1. ....

2. ....

3. ....

I'M GRATEFUL FOR: **DATE:**

1. ....

2. ....

3. ....

I'M GRATEFUL FOR: **DATE:**

1. ....

2. ....

3. ....

I'M GRATEFUL FOR: **DATE:**

1. ....

2. ....

3. ....

I'M GRATEFUL FOR: **DATE:**

1. ....

2. ....

3. ....

I'm GRATEFUL Every Day

> *"When you rise in the morning, give thanks for the light, for your life, for your strength."*
> – Tecumseh

I'M GRATEFUL FOR: **DATE:**

1. _____

2. _____

3. _____

I'M GRATEFUL FOR: **DATE:**

1. _____

2. _____

3. _____

I'M GRATEFUL FOR: **DATE:**

1. _____

2. _____

3. _____

I'M GRATEFUL FOR: **DATE:**

1. ....

2. ....

3. ....

I'M GRATEFUL FOR: **DATE:**

1. _____

2. _____

3. _____

I'M GRATEFUL FOR: **DATE:**

1. _____

2. ....

3. _____

I'M GRATEFUL FOR: **DATE:**

1. ....

2. ....

3. ....

I'm GRATEFUL Every Day

My Favorite Quote:

I'M GRATEFUL FOR: **DATE:**

1. _____

2. _____

3. _____

I'M GRATEFUL FOR: **DATE:**

1. _____

2. _____

3. _____

I'M GRATEFUL FOR: **DATE:**

1. _____

2. _____

3. _____

I'M GRATEFUL FOR: **DATE:**

1. _____

2. _____

3. _____

I'M GRATEFUL FOR: **DATE:**

1. _____

2. _____

3. _____

I'M GRATEFUL FOR: **DATE:**

1. _____

2. _____

3. _____

I'M GRATEFUL FOR: **DATE:**

1. _____

2. _____

3. _____

Made in the USA
Las Vegas, NV
05 February 2022

43126022R00065